Dig in!

Written by Samantha Montgomerie
Illustrated by Jiarui Jiang

Collins

Pop cuts off the tops.

Min can toss the tops in the pot.

The hens peck.

4

A dog runs up.

Pop tips the bits in the bin.

6

Min puffs and digs.

Min tips the sack up.

Pop pats the mud.

Min ticks.

The pods get big.

The pods fill the bag.

12

Min and Pop tuck in.

13

/b/

14

🐾 Review: After reading 🐾

Use your assessment from hearing the children read to choose any GPCs, words or tricky words that need additional practice.

Read 1: Decoding

- Ask the children to read pages 2 and 3. Encourage them to blend in their heads as they read these words. Focus on the word **Pop**. What other names do the children know for older relatives or friends? (e.g. *Gramps, Grandpa, Gran, Nanna*)
- Read pages 7 and 12. Ask the children to point to the /f/ sound on each page. Discuss how 'f' and 'ff' make the same sound.
- Look at the "I spy sounds" pages (14–15) together. Ask the children to point out as many things that they can in the picture that begin with the /b/ sound. (*bicycle, birds, butterflies, bees, bag, badges, boots, bush, ball, boy, bull, bucket*)

Read 2: Prosody

- Read pages 4 and 5 in a bland voice and then again in an excited storyteller voice.
  - Ask them which reading they preferred and why. Encourage the children to read the main sentences in an excited voice.
  - Ask the children to try different voices for the dog's bark, so that the dog sounds excited, too.

Read 3: Comprehension

- Ask the children to describe any fruit or vegetables they have seen growing. Talk about any compost bins they have seen and how food waste, like carrot peel, can help other vegetables or fruit grow.
- Talk about the different things Pop and Min do during the story. Ask questions, such as:
  - On page 4: What do the hens peck? (e.g. *the carrot tops*)
  - On page 8: What did Min and Pop do? (e.g. *they planted seeds*)
  - On pages 10–11: Do you think it took a long time for the pods to grow? Why? (e.g. *yes – Min ticked lots of days off a calendar*)